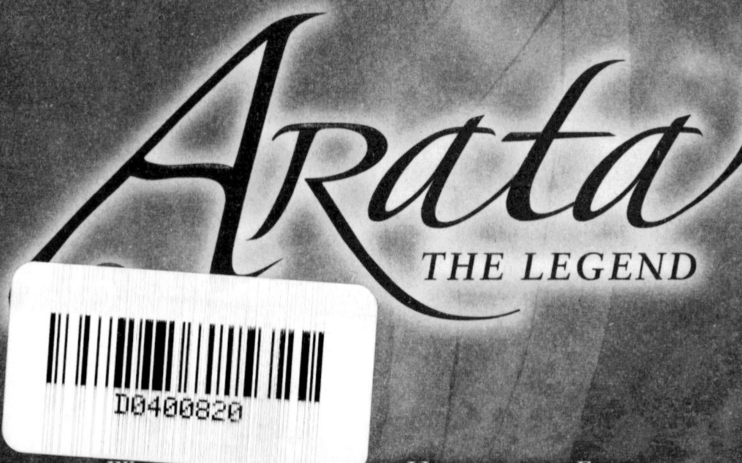

D0400820

We are Man, born of Heaven and Earth,
Moon and Sun and everything under them.

Eyes, Ears, Nose, Tongue, Body, Mind...

Purity will pierce evil and
open up the world of darkness.

All life will be reborn and invigorated.

Appear now.

STORY & ART BY

Yuu Watase

Arata
THE LEGEND

CHARACTERS

Arata

young man who elongs to the Hime Clan. He wanders to Kando Forest and ds up in present-day pan after switching places with Arata Hinohara.

Arata Hinohara

A kindhearted high school freshman. Betrayed by a trusted friend, he stumbles through a secret portal into another world and becomes a Hayagami-wielding Sho.

The People of Amawakuni in a Distant World

Kotoha
A girl from the Uneme Clan who serves Arata. She possesses the mysterious power to heal wounds.

Kannagi
One of the Twelve Shinsho. He has a Hayagami called "Homura."

Princess Kikuri
The ruling princess of Amawakuni. She hovers near death after being attacked by her vassals, the Twelve Shinsho.

The Story Thus Far

In a distant world, Princess Kikuri prepares to ordain a successor after her sixty-year reign. Hime Clan member Arata poses for the role, but during the ceremony, the Twelve Shinsho attempt to murder Princess Kikuri! Arata manages to escape with his life, but the assassins pin the crime on him. Hunted and alone, he flees into a mysterious forest where he is swallowed up by a giant tree.

Meanwhile in present-day Japan, Arata Hinohara begins high school. He is bullied, and his only friend betrays him. Feeling hopeless, Hinohara wanders down an alley and passes into the other world. There, Hinohara learns that he and the other Arata have somehow switched places. While defending himself against Princess Kikuri's true attacker, Kannagi, Hinohara discovers that he is a Sho—the master of a godlike weapon called a "Hayagami." Unfortunately, Hinohara is captured and sent to the fearsome island of Gatoya...

CONTENTS

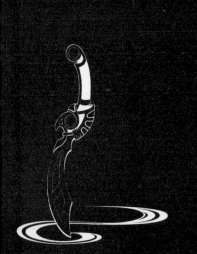

CHAPTER 8
GATOYA

WHAT ARE YOU DOING?! THAT'S CRUEL!!
NO, LOOK! A SHO AND HIS HAYAGAMI ARE ONE, SO YOU CAN PLACE IT ANYWHERE IN YOUR BODY.
Huh?
IT DOESN'T HURT... BUT STOP IT!
YOU'LL GET USED TO IT IN NO TIME.
CHAPTER 8
GATOYA

A HOLE IN THE MIDDLE OF THE OCEAN?! IT'S AN ABYSS...

YOU'RE ON YOUR OWN NOW! YOU'LL NEVER LEAVE THIS PLACE...
IT'S A WARPED AREA!
!!
TCH...

KOTOHA, WHAT DID THAT GUY MEAN BY "WARPED AREA"?
It's kind of hot...
HM... ALL I KNOW IS THAT PEOPLE CALL THIS PLACE THE HELL AT THE END OF THE WORLD.
THE END OF THE WORLD?! THEN THE CAPITAL WHERE THE PRINCESS IS...
OH, IT'S AT LEAST THIS FAR AWAY! MAYBE...
NO USE ASKING KOTOHA ABOUT GEOGRAPHY.
SIGH
THIS CAN'T BE HAPPENING...
IT'S LIKE WHEN THE HERO IN AN RPG GETS HIT ON THE HEAD AND EVERYTHING GOES ALL CRAZY...
BUT...
"I BELIEVE IN YOU."
"I'LL BRING THIS HAYAGAMI...
...TO YOU, PRINCESS!"

FIRST WE HAVE TO GET OUT OF HERE! SOMEHOW...
SIGH
THOSE GUYS THAT FRAMED ME SENT ME TO THIS PLACE...
MASTER ARATA...!
I'LL NEVER FORGIVE THEM!!
THE TWELVE SHINSHO!

DOOM
IT'S NOT HERE ...
...AFTER ALL.

THERE'S NO RECORD OF THAT HAYAGAMI OR ITS KAMUI.
IF IT EXISTED, IT SHOULD HAVE BEEN RECORDED HERE.
DOES THAT MEAN A NEW HAYAGAMI HAS BEEN FOUND?
A HAYAGAMI WITH THE POWER TO REJECT MY HOMURA...
...
KANNAGI!
YOU'RE OBSESSED WITH THE HAYAGAMI. WHAT MORE DO YOU NEED TO KNOW ABOUT THEM?
IT'S NOT OBSESSION. IT'S LOVE.
WHENEVER YOU VISIT THE IMPERIAL COURT, YOU ALWAYS COME HERE.
WIP
...
NOW THAT PRINCESS KIKURI HAS FALLEN, THE TWELVE SHINSHO MUST STAND UNITED.

DON'T GO OFF DOING ANYTHING ON YOUR OWN.
OF COURSE, LORD AKACHI.

EVERYONE IS RETURNING TO THEIR FIEFS FOR NOW, RIGHT?
I SHALL DO THE SAME.

W... WHAT IS IT?

A TEENAGE BOY...AND GIRL...

I GUESS THE MORE PEOPLE THERE ARE...
mumble
?
HEY! HEY! HEY!!

FWOOO
SH
MOVE! MOVE!!
SH
?!

FWIP
HEY! SHH! SHH!
FWIP
Tch.
NOT THOSE TWO BRATS AGAIN...
WHEN THEY GET RILED UP, THEY'RE DANGER-OUS. LEAVE THEM BE.
SHP
UH-OH...
THESE GUYS LOOK LIKE TROUBLE.
His hair's bright red.
NEW-COMERS, EH?!

Hmm...
WEIRD CLOTHES!
OGLE
YEAH, WEIRD CLOTHES !!
OGLE
THE PERSON WHO DESIGNED THIS UNIFORM WOULDN'T APPRECIATE THAT.
OGLE
HEY!!!
ZANG
?!
SHE'S ADORABLE !!
BEDAZZLED
HEY! THAT GIRL'S REALLY PRETTY!
WSP
I KNOW! I KNOW !!
N...
NICE CURVES TOO!
WHAT? I DIDN'T GET THAT FAR!
WSP
NOW'S OUR CHANCE.
WIP
HEY! HEY!!
WHAT NOW?

GIVE US YOUR CLOTHES AND ALL YOUR STUFF!!
YEAH!!
PUSHED AROUND AGAIN...
Sigh
I GUESS THERE ARE BULLIES WHER-EVER YOU GO.
WHAT?!
TUG
WHAT'S THE BIG IDEA?! CUT IT OUT!!
HAND IT OVER!!
N-NO!
YOU'VE GOT GUTS TO DEFY US.
!
BUT I'LL SHOW YOU WHAT HAPPENS ...
TMP

...TO PEOPLE WHO DON'T OBEY!!
WHOA!
SH
THESE GUYS...
...ARE SERIOUSLY...
YAH!
TAKE IT EASY!

SWIP
...TRYING TO KILL ME!
THAT KID DODGES PRETTY GOOD.
HEY! YOU TWO ARE A JOKE!
WHUP
WHAT'S WRONG, COWARDS?
AFRAID TO FIGHT ME ONE ON ONE?
I MISSED...
LET'S GO, KOTO-HA.
KRK
DON'T TAKE ME...

...LIGHTLY !!
FLASH
AH...
FWIK

OH NO!!
IT'S STARTING!
THE HOUR OF RECKONING!
WE CAN'T STAY HERE, BRO! LET'S GO!
I WON'T FORGET THIS!
HUH?!
HEY, WHAT'S GOING ON?
RUN!!
AHH!

WHO
GAH!!
!!

WHAT ...?!
IT... SWAL-LOWED HIM?
AAAAH!!

EEEE...
WOOSH
IT SUCKED HIM IN!
WHAT JUST HAPPENED?!
THE RECKONING.
ONCE AGAIN...
SHIVER
...WARDEN TSUTSUGA HAS PASSED JUDGMENT!
WARDEN TSUTSUGA?
JUDGMENT?!

CHAPTER 9
UNEME
WHAT'S WARDEN TSU-TSUGA'S JUDG-MENT?!
THANK GOODNESS... THE RECKONING IS OVER FOR TODAY.
EXCUSE ME! WHAT WAS THAT JUST NOW?!
WUZZ
WUZZ
A MAN GOT SUCKED INTO THAT TUBE!
AND WHO'S WARDEN TSU-TSUGA?
DIDN'T THEY TELL YOU ANYTHING ABOUT THIS PLACE?

WARDEN TSUTSUGA IS THE OVERSEER HERE AT GATOYA, THE ISLAND OF EXILE.
HE PASSES JUDGMENT ONCE A DAY, JUST AS YOU SAW.
TWO PRISONERS ARE CHOSEN AMONG US PRISONERS AND TAKEN AWAY.
WE NEVER KNOW WHO WILL BE CHOSEN...
...BUT THE HOUR OF RECKONING COMES UPON US EVERY SINGLE DAY WITHOUT ANY WARNING.
W-WHAT HAP-PENS TO THOSE WHO GET TAKEN?
NOBODY KNOWS. THEY NEVER COME BACK. EXECU-TION'S MY GUESS.
THOSE WHO CAN'T STAND THE SUSPENSE EITHER JUMP OFF A CLIFF OR HANG THEM-SELVES.
I was spared.
We're safe now... for today.
TH...

YOU MEAN EVERYBODY HERE LIVES IN CONSTANT FEAR OF *THE RECKONING*?!
W-WE HAVE TO GET OUT OF HERE QUICK!!

"EXILE HIM TO GA-TOYA."
KANNAGI... THAT SADISTIC JERK!

SO THAT'S WHY THEY CALL THIS THE HELL AT THE END OF THE WORLD...
WOBBLE
I FEEL SICK TO MY STOM-ACH.

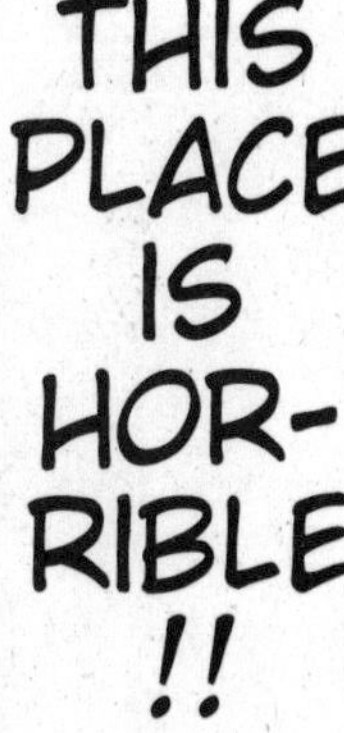
THIS PLACE IS HOR-RIBLE!!

CHT-CHT-CHT

SHOOM
?!
SPLAT

HEH
LOOK, HE'S SCARED.
HEH HEH HEH
THE NEW-COMER'S A WIMP!
HE WAS JUST SHOWING OFF TO THE GIRL EARLIER.
THOSE GUYS ...
THROB
WHAT, ARE YOU UPSET? COME ON UP HERE THEN!
LET'S GO, KOTOHA!!
HUH ?
TUG
MASTER ARATA, YOU'RE GOING SO FAST!
HOW DARE HE THROW SOMETHING INTO MY HAIR! I HAVEN'T EVEN BEEN ABLE TO TAKE A BATH, AND NOW...!!
HEH HEH...

OH...

I THINK WE'RE LOST, MASTER ARATA.

TCH! WHERE'D THEY GO?!

SWIP

SORRY... I WAS KINDA IRRITA-TED ...

HEY, WHAT'S THE BIG IDEA?!

Apologize when you bump into some-one!

I barely touched you.

EVERYONE SEEMS TO BE ON EDGE.

THOOM
THOOM
THOOM
BUT HOW ARE WE GOING TO GET OUT OF HERE?!
WE'LL FIND A WAY, MASTER ARATA!
ANY IDEA HOW?

SLUMP

IT'S NO GOOD. AT THIS RATE, WE'LL NEVER MAKE IT.

WE'LL DIE OF STRESS BEFORE ***WARDEN TSUTSUGA'S JUDGMENT*** GETS US.

SW OO

I JUST PROMISED TO DELIVER THIS HAYAGAMI TO THE PRIN-CESS... WHY AM I WASTING TIME LIKE THIS?

I MEAN, DO SOMETHING, HAYAGAMI. YOU'RE A GOD, AREN'T YOU?!

SHHK

OW! OH, FOR CRYIN' OUT LOUD!

PEEK

MASTER ARATA! I FOUND SOMETHING GREAT!

LOOK!
THE PIPES ARE CONNECTED TO AN UNDER-GROUND WATER VEIN!
HOT WATER!
PLUP

WHY DON'T YOU TAKE A BATH?
OH... IS IT OKAY IF I GO FIRST?
OF COURSE!
WOW, A BATH! A REAL BATH! IT'S BEEN AGES!

I NEVER MISSED A BATH BACK IN JAPAN.
BEING CLEAN IS SO IMPORTANT.

SERIOUSLY, I FEEL LIKE I WAS ON THE VERGE OF LOSING SOME OF MY HUMANITY.
Like a manga artist facing an editorial deadline.

EEEEK!
SPLASH
SWIP

WAIT... WHAT?! DON'T TELL ME YOU AND ARATA ARE THAT CLOSE!
With a face like that?
IMAGINATION RUNNING WILD
I AM YOUR UNEME! I'VE SERVED YOU SINCE I WAS A CHILD!
UNEME?
YOU REALLY HAVE LOST YOUR MEMORY, HUH!
THROB
UNGH...
WHAT'S WRONG?
OH, IT'S NOTHING.
AH, THAT'S EASY.
SHEEN
LET ME SEE!
?

IT'S HEALED!
WOW! HOW'D YOU DO THAT?!
THE WOMEN OF THE UNEME CLAN HAVE THE POWER TO HEAL. IT HELPS US PROTECT THE HIME CLAN, WHOM WE SERVE.
I'VE ALWAYS HEALED YOUR MINOR SCRAPES.
But you probably don't remember.
WE SHARE THE SAME BIRTHDAY, MASTER ARATA. I WAS BORN TO SERVE YOU.
SWUFF
HMM... SO THEY'RE NOT SWEET-HEARTS OR ANY-THING.

BA-BUMP
W-WHAT?!
RELAX. I'M DOING A CLEANSING ON YOU NOW. IT'S MORE EFFECTIVE IF I TOUCH YOUR BARE SKIN.
?!
WMM
AHH...
WMM
WMM
WMM
IT FEELS...
...WARM ...

JUST LIKE ...
...MY MOTHER ...
DO YOU FEEL MORE AT PEACE NOW?

WE UNEME DON'T JUST HEAL EXTERNAL INJURIES.
Now, have a nice soak.
I FEEL SO RELAXED.
AHHH
AND THE EXHAUSTION SEEMS TO BE GONE.
...
SHE'S AMAZING.
SHE MAY BE AN UNEME, BUT IT STILL HAD TO BE SCARY FOR HER TO FOLLOW ME TO A PLACE LIKE THIS.
AND HERE I AM, ACTING SO HELPLESS...
HEY, KOTOHA! THANK—
VHOOM

THOOM
KREK
THOOM
THE HOUR OF RECKONING !!
KREK
KREK
KOTOHA!! OVER HERE!!
THOOM

BAAAH!!
KOTOHA !!
WOOSH

KOTOHA!!
KLAT...
Unh...
MASTER... ARATA...
KLAK

CHAPTER 10
THE SEARCH

KOTOHA!!

NO! THE TUBE'S MOVED, AND ITS OPENING IS CLOSED!
I HAVE TO FIND HER!!

DASH

PLEASE BE OKAY!!

"MASTER ARATA..."

IF SOMETHING HAPPENS TO HER, IT'LL BE ALL MY FAULT!

THIS PLACE IS TOO DANGEROUS! FORGIVE ME, KOTOHA!!

WIP

HOW DO I GET DOWN THERE?

GEEZ... IT'S LIKE A MAZE!

THIS SPACE REALLY IS WARPED...

OH
SWF
SWF
AH!
THUMP
WHAK
WHAK
WHO ARE YOU?!
A... MARKET-PLACE ?!
ON AN ISLAND OF EXILED CRIMI-NALS ?!

I DON'T WANT TO HAVE ANYTHING TO DO WITH THESE PEOPLE, BUT I HAVE NO CHOICE.
EXCUSE ME, I'M LOOKING FOR A GIRL.

SHE FELL THROUGH A HOLE UP ABOVE! I'M WORRIED ABOUT HER.
HAVEN'T SEEN HER.

GATOYA HAS COUNTLESS COMPLEX LEVELS.
BUT THE GROUND IS SOFT AND THE LEVELS AREN'T TOO HIGH. SHE PROBABLY SURVIVED.

PHEW
TH-THANK YOU!

WHUP
?

I GAVE YOU INFORMATION! NOW PAY UP!
BARTERING IS A WAY OF LIFE HERE!

RUMMAGE RUMMAGE

GIMME A SECOND!

I MAY NEED THIS SWEATER LATER...

MY CELL PHONE AND IPOD ARE DEFINITELY OUT!

I NEED MY HAIR GEL AND MIRROR...

TRAIN PASS, WALLET, STATIONERY...

A COLOR MARKER!

WHAT'S THIS?
SEE? LOOK AT THE PRETTY COLOR YOU CAN WRITE IN!
SKRIK SKRIK
OOOH
THIS IS AMAZING!!
Hey!
TOO BAD THE INK'S RUNNING LOW.
IF THAT'S HOW THINGS WORK HERE...
HELP YOU LOOK FOR A GIRL? WHY SHOULD I?

TA-
DAH
I'LL GIVE YOU MY VIDEO MEMBERSHIP CARD!
HUH?! WHAT'S THAT? I'VE NEVER SEEN ONE OF THOSE BEFORE!
I'M LOOKING FOR INFORMATION. HERE'S A FRESH NEW TEN YEN COIN!
A PLASTIC BOTTLE!
EMPTY
OOH!

HEY, DID YOU HEAR?!
SOME NEW KID'S GOT A LOT OF NEVER-BEFORE-SEEN STUFF TO TRADE!!
BZZ
WHAT?!

HEY!!
I HAVE INFORMATION. MANTA ON LEVEL 13 AND HAJI ON LEVEL 2 HAVE A THING GOING ON!
YOU CALL THAT A TIP?!
HEY, I'VE NEVER SEEN SHOES LIKE THOSE BEFORE!
YOU CAN'T HAVE MY SNEAK-ERS!
TUG
TUG
Ow!
NOT MY WATCH!!
STOP THAT!!
TMP
IF YOU DON'T CUT THAT OUT RIGHT NOW, I WON'T TRADE YOU ANY MORE BOOZE!
OSOME!
A WOMAN?

UNH...
OH!
SHE'S AWAKE!
DON'T TRY TO MOVE!
OH!!
YOU SCARED US! THERE WAS A LOUD BANG, SO WE PEEKED OUT AND...
KANATE! HERE'S THE WATER!
WHERE AM I?

DON'T BE SCARED. THIS IS OUR FORT!
Have some water.
THANK YOU... BUT WHY DID YOU SAVE ME?
WHAT DO I DO? I HOPE MASTER ARATA IS ALL RIGHT BY HIMSELF.
WELL, UM...
HEH HEH HEH
What are you smirking about ?!
WHAM
?
SO YOUR NAME'S ARATA, EH? WANT SOMETHING TO DRINK?
A COKE...
...BUT I GUESS YOU WOULDN'T HAVE THAT. WATER'S FINE.

SO YOU'RE LOOKING FOR A GIRL, HUH?
STILL, YOU SHOULDN'T GO AROUND FLASHING ALL YOUR STUFF.
OH... GOT IT...
Here, snacks. On the house.
Thank you.
I WAS SURPRISED TO SEE PEOPLE DOING BUSINESS HERE.
WELL, WE HAVE TO SURVIVE SOME-HOW.
HA HA
BUT YOU NEVER KNOW WHEN YOU'LL BE SNATCHED UP BY WARDEN TSUTSUGA'S JUDGMENT AND EXECUTED, RIGHT?

A SHO IS THE MASTER OF A HAYAGAMI.
TSUTSUGA USES ITS KAMUI TO RULE THIS PRISON ISLAND OF GATOYA.
HAYA-GAMI?!
THEN THAT WAS KAMUI TOO?!
NO ONE CAN DEFY A SHO'S POWER.
I WISH ANOTHER SHO WOULD COME AND SAVE US.
GACK
THEY SAY THE ONLY ONE WHO CAN DEFEAT WARDEN TSUTSUGA IS ANOTHER SHO...
...BUT WHY WOULD A SHO COME TO A PLACE LIKE THIS?!
BA-BUMP BA-BUMP BA-BUMP
What's the matter?
I HAVE TO GO.
Thanks for the food.
REALLY? OH, WAIT...

HERE, TAKE THIS MAP!

HUH?!

THERE WAS ONCE A MAN WHO SECRETLY SURVEYED ALL OF GATOYA BECAUSE HE WANTED TO ESCAPE.

...BUT HE GOT TAKEN, SO YOU CAN HAVE IT.

THANK YOU! OH, YEAH. I'D BETTER GIVE YOU SOME-THING.

SWF

NO NEED.

GOOD LUCK FINDING YOUR GIRL, ARATA!

THAT'S WHY I GAVE IT TO HIM.
I KNOW HOW IT FEELS TO LOSE SOMEONE ...
SORRY!
WHAT'LL I DO? I NEVER IMAGINED THERE'D BE A SHO HERE.
I GUESS I'LL HAVE TO FIGHT THIS TSUTSUGA IF I EVER WANT TO GET OFF THIS ISLAND!
I HAVE TO HURRY UP AND FIND KOTOHA AND...
?!
HEY... THE MAP!
THAT GUY!!

IT'S NO USE... I CAN'T FIND KOTOHA.

I MANAGED TO GET A MAP, ONLY TO HAVE IT STOLEN ...

WHAT THE HECK AM I DOING?!

THERE'S NO WAY I CAN SCALE A CLIFF LIKE THIS.

I CAN'T EVEN START LOOKING FOR TSUTSUGA. I'M BOXED IN ON ALL SIDES.

"I WISH ANOTHER SHO WOULD COME AND SAVE US."

HAYA-GAMI!!

ZHEEN

APPEAR !!

UNH...

GEEZ!
I'M SUPPOSED TO BE A CHOSEN SHO, BUT I CAN'T DO ANYTHING!
"I..."
"...BELIEVE IN YOU."
I'M SORRY, PRINCESS.
IT'S TOO MUCH FOR ME...
IS THAT ...
...A HAYAGAMI?

?!
WHO'S HE?!

CHAPTER 11

KANATE & GINCHI

IS HE AN EXILED CRIMINAL ?
BUT HOW DID HE KNOW THIS IS A HAYAGAMI ?
COULD HE BE... TSUTSUGA ?!
THERE MUST BE SOME MISTAKE. HOW CAN I BE A SHO? THIS HAYAGAMI WON'T DO ANYTHING I SAY!
AND NOW I'VE LOST MY FRIEND.
I CAN'T DO ANYTHING RIGHT IN THIS WORLD.

I AM JUST ANOTHER EXILE.

BUT YOU LOOKED TROUBLED ...

KLINK

HUH?

I WAS AFRAID YOU WOULD JUMP.

WOOOOO

I'M NOT THAT BRAVE.

NO? BUT YOU'RE A SHO. YOU CONTROL A HAYAGAMI.

THAT'S ...

I MADE A PROMISE TO THE PRINCESS, BUT I CAN'T...

A PROMISE TO THE PRINCESS?

I WANT YOU TO GOVERN THIS WORLD IN MY PLACE.
I NEED YOU TO BRING THAT HAYAGAMI TO ME BEFORE LIFE LEAVES MY BODY ENTIRELY.
THE PRINCESS MUST'VE BEEN CRAZY...
...TO THINK SOMEBODY LIKE ME COULD GOVERN THIS WORLD.
IT'S NOT LIKE ASKING SOMEBODY TO BE STUDENT BODY PRESIDENT.
And even that's too much for me.
ANYWAY, THERE'S NO WAY I CAN CLIMB A WALL LIKE THIS. IT'S ALL OVER.
YES.
AS LONG AS YOU BELIEVE IT'S IMPOSSIBLE, IT WILL BE.
GULP

WHEN YOU'RE LOST, CALM DOWN AND TAKE A GOOD LOOK AT EVERYTHING THAT'S BEFORE YOUR EYES— EVERYTHING IN ITS ENTIRETY.
THEN THE ANSWER... WHAT YOU CAN ACHIEVE WILL BECOME TRULY CLEAR.
?!
BUT TELL ME, WHY DID YOU MAKE SUCH A BIG PROMISE TO THE PRINCESS?
WELL...
"I BELIEVE IN YOU."
I GUESS...
...I WAS REALLY HAPPY...
...THAT SHE BELIEVED IN ME!

YOU WANT TO BE WORTHY OF HER TRUST. THAT'S NO EASY TASK.

BUT I'M SURE YOU WILL SUCCEED.

BA-BUMP

"YOU WILL SUCCEED" ...

SHH

HE'S GONE?

He didn't fall, did he?

WHO WAS THAT GUY?

AND WHY WAS I RAMBLING ON LIKE THAT?

I DON'T EVEN KNOW WHETHER HE WAS FRIEND OR FOE.

WMM

IT'S NOT SAFE TO TRUST ANYBODY HERE.

BUT...

"CALM DOWN..."

"...AND TAKE A GOOD LOOK..."

"...AT EVERY-THING THAT'S BEFORE YOUR EYES..."

OH!

THAT'S...
KOTOHA!!
BUT WHAT'S SHE DOING WITH THAT RED-HAIRED GUY?!
OH!
DRAM
THANK GOODNESS! AT LEAST SHE'S ALIVE!
TMP
TMP
TAKE A GOOD LOOK... AT EVERY-THING IN ITS ENTIRETY.
THAT'S RIGHT. I'LL ONLY GET LOST IF I RUN AROUND BLINDLY.
IN ORDER TO GET TO THAT LOCA-TION...
KLIK KLIK KLIK

I GOT A LOOK AT THAT MAP, SO... HERE...?
THE CORRIDOR I PASSED WAS HERE, WHICH MEANS...
I GO THIS WAY!

So...
YOUR NAME IS KOTOHA!

EVEN YOUR NAME IS PRETTY! I'M KANATE!
AND I'M GINCHI, HIS PROTÉGÉ.
OH...

UM... I HAVE TO GET BACK TO MASTER ARATA...
YOU MUST BE HUNGRY, HUH?!
I'LL GO TO THE MARKET-PLACE AND TRADE FOR SOME FOOD!

WHIP

I WANNA MAKE KANATE LOOK GOOD.

I'VE BEEN HANGING ON TO THIS, BUT I'LL TRADE IT FOR LOTS OF FOOD AND STUFF SHE'LL LIKE!

WHAP

WH

AM

?!

KLINK
LET'S SEE...
IF THAT PIPE IS OVER THERE, THEN... THIS MUST BE THE RIGHT LEVEL.
KLIK KLIK
NOBODY KNOWS WHERE THEIR HIDEOUT IS...
...AND THAT REDHEAD KANATE IS SCARY WHEN HE GETS MAD! HE'S BEATEN A BUNCH OF GUYS HALF TO DEATH BEFORE.
VEEN
A RED-HAIRED BOY AND HIS PART-NER?
OH, YOU MEAN KANATE AND GINCHI!
KLIK KLIK
KLIK KLIK
You're wasting lead.
HEH HEH
SHE'S WITH A COUPLE OF DANGER-OUS CRETINS?!
HEH HEH
IMAGINATION RUNNING WILD (GONE-TOO-FAR VERSION)
KLIK KLIK KLIK
Huh? No more?
KOTOHA !!

BA-BUMP
BA-BUMP

THIS ISN'T GOING SO GOOD. I DON'T KNOW WHAT TO SAY TO HER.
FWUP
FWUP
WIP
I WONDER IF MASTER ARATA'S ALL RIGHT...

HUH?! OH, YOU DON'T HAVE TO CALL ME "MASTER."
I SAID "MASTER ARATA"! YOU KNOW, THE BOY I WAS WITH. I'M WORRIED ABOUT HIM.
OH! FORGET THAT GUY! HE'S A WEAKLING.
HE JUST DUCKS AND DODGES AND WON'T FIGHT. HE WON'T LAST LONG IN THIS PLACE!
MMH
YOU'RE BETTER OFF WITH US!

MASTER ARATA ISN'T WEAK! HIS TRUE STRENGTH ...
IN THIS WORLD, BEING STRONG MEANS BEING A SHO!
SH A
APPEAR !!
HMPH! IF ONLY THIS WAS A HAYAGAMI ...
SIGH
AND THE TWELVE SHINSHO ARE AWESOME! I WISH I COULD BE A SHO!
WELL, ACTUALLY, MASTER ARATA IS—
WORD HAS IT THAT TSUTSUGA, THE ONE WHO PASSES JUDGMENT HERE, IS A SHO.
STOP TALKING ABOUT THAT GUY!!
GINCHI'S LATE. I'D BETTER CHECK ON HIM. STAY RIGHT THERE!
GEEZ... WHAT DOES SHE SEE IN THAT GUY ANYWAY ?!

WHUMP
OH, SORRY ...

HEY!!

NEVER! SHE'S MINE!

YOU!!
WHERE'S KOTOHA?! GIVE HER BACK TO ME!!

WHAT?!
PERFECT TIMING. LET'S CONTINUE WHERE WE LEFT OFF. IF YOU WANT THE GIRL, YOU'LL HAVE TO FIGHT ME FOR HER!
I DON'T KNOW WHO YOU ARE, "MASTER ARATA"...
BUT TO ME, YOU'RE JUST A COWARD!
GRR
HYAH!!
DON'T DODGE! FIGHT ME, YOU CHICKEN!!
...!!

A SWORD?! WHERE DID HE ...?
GIVE ME BACK KOTOHA !!

IF YOU DON'T...
KLANK
...I'M REALLY GONNA—
SH
YOU'RE REALLY GONNA WHAT?!
THERE'S NO WAY YOU CAN BEAT ME WITH THAT RUSTY OLD PIECE OF JUNK!

KLANG
UGH!!
WHIP

ENOUGH ALREADY! WHERE'S KOTOHA?!

Heh.
WHAT? YOU LOVE HER OR SOMETHING?
WHAT'S THE BIG DEAL? SHE'S JUST A GIRL.
IT'S NOT LIKE THAT!!

SHE'S BEEN SAVING ME AND ENCOURAGING ME ...
...EVER SINCE I CAME TO THIS WORLD!
NOW IT'S MY TURN TO SAVE HER!!
I'LL PROTECT HER NO MATTER WHAT!! NOW GIVE HER BACK TO ME!!
GULP

?!
WH...
HUH?
GINCHI?!

CHAPTER 12
THE RING

GINCHI!!
WHAT HAPPENED?! YOU'RE HURT!
KANATE...
IT'S NOTHING. JUST A SCRATCH.
I JUST TRIPPED AND FELL.
BUT... WHO DID THIS TO YOU?!
UNH...

ZANG
ARATA, OUR DUEL WILL HAVE TO WAIT!!
HUH?
YOU'RE THE ONE WHO ATTACKED ME.
WIP
Hang in there!!
MASTER ARATA...
I'M BACK.
WHAT HAPPENED TO YOU TWO?!
VWP
AN ENTRYWAY IN A PLACE LIKE THIS?
MASTER ARATA!!
KOTOHA!!

I WAS SO WORRIED! ARE YOU ALL RIGHT?!
WHAT ABOUT YOU, KOTOHA? DID THOSE GUYS DO SOMETHING, ER, ANYTHING TO YOU?!

SOME-THING? ANYTHING? WHAT DO YOU MEAN EXACTLY?
AGH!! I MEAN ...
Er... Um...

KANATE, YOU'RE HURTING ME!!
OH
LET ME SEE YOUR WOUND!
MAYBE I'M THE ONLY ONE WHO'S GOT HIS MIND IN THE GUTTER ...
REGRETFUL

IT'S ALL RIGHT! I CAN HEAL THIS EASILY WITH MY UNEME POWERS.
I WAS CARELESS. I DIDN'T EXPECT TO MEET THEM ON OUR SECRET ROUTE.
THEM?

ONE TIME I BEAT SOME GUYS UP AND BROKE A BUNCH OF THEIR BONES. THEN I PULLED OUT THEIR HAIR AND SCRAWLED STUFF ON THEIR FACES.
EVER SINCE THEN, THEY'VE HAD IT IN FOR US!
WHO COULD BLAME THEM?
SORRY, KANATE.

THOSE GUYS WAITED TIL I WASN'T AROUND TO AMBUSH YOU!
THEY'LL PAY FOR THAT!
!!
I WAS GONNA TRADE THE RING FOR SOME NICE STUFF...
...BUT THEY TOOK IT.
Eh heh...
YOU WAIT HERE! I'LL BEAT THE SNOT OUT OF 'EM!
AND I'LL GET THE RING BACK TOO!
KANATE!
SHK SHK
BAM
Ow!
TMP TMP
KANATE MUST CARE FOR YOU VERY MUCH.
HUH?
I-I GUESS.

BEFORE I WAS SENT HERE TO GATOYA, I HUNG OUT WITH A GANG OF THIEVES AND GOT INTO ALL KINDS OF TROUBLE.
KANATE WAS IN THAT GROUP. HE'S TWO YEARS OLDER THAN ME, AND HE'S ALWAYS LOOKED OUT FOR ME.

WHEN THE LAW WAS CATCHING UP TO US, FOR SOME REASON IT WAS KANATE AND I WHO HAD TO TAKE THE RAP.
BUT WHY WERE YOU IN THAT GANG? WHAT ABOUT YOUR FAMILY?

WHO KNOWS?
THOSE BANDITS ATTACKED MY FAMILY WHILE WE WERE TRAVELING AND CARRIED ME OFF. I DON'T KNOW WHAT HAPPENED TO THEM.

THAT RING WAS THE ONLY THING I HAD OF MY MOM'S.

...
BUT I'VE ALWAYS HAD KANATE! WE'RE LIKE ONE!
SOME-DAY WE'RE GONNA GET OUT OF HERE TOGETH-ER!

THANKS FOR THE HELP, KOTOHA! IT FEELS A LOT BETTER!

WHUP WHUP

IT'S BEEN A LONG TIME, BUT IT ALMOST FELT LIKE MY MOM WAS HOLDING ME.

Eh heh...

THEY'VE ONLY HAD EACH OTHER FOR SUCH A LONG TIME...

MAYBE THEY'RE NOT AS BAD AS I THOUGHT ...

THIS PLACE IS RULED BY A SHO NAMED TSUTSUGA. HE HAS A HAYAGAMI!

WE HAVE TO FIND HIM AND DO SOMETHING, OR WE'LL BE STUCK HERE FOR THE REST OF OUR LIVES!

KLINK

THOSE BALLS CLATTER AND WARN US WHENEVER THERE'S THE SLIGHTEST MOVEMENT!!
THE HOUR OF RECKONING IS COMING!! I'M GONNA FIND KANATE!!
KLAK KLANK
KLAK KLAK
THE HOUR OF RECKONING?!
MASTER ARATA! LET'S HELP HIM FIND KANATE!
THOSE TWO SAVED MY LIFE!
KOTOHA...
I DON'T FEEL ANY VIBRATIONS OR HEAR ANYTHING...
FWIP

BUT WHERE IS TSUTSUGA?! I COULDN'T FIND HIM EVEN FROM THE OUTSIDE.
THE ONLY WAY TO FIND OUT IS ...
UH-UH! NO WAY!! I CAN'T GET SUCKED UP ON PURPOSE!!
WIP WIP
OH!
GINCHI! WHERE'S KANATE?!
I STILL DON'T ...
WAH!!
KRASH
GASP

HAH!
YOU GUYS ARE NOTHING!
THE CRIME OF HURTING GINCHI IS WORSE THAN ALL THE PAST CRIMES YOU'VE COMMITTED!!
THANK GOOD-NESS!
GINCHI!!
STOMP
Urk
HERE!
IT'S YOUR MOTHER'S RING! TAKE GOOD CARE OF IT!
HUH?
KANATE!!
KANATE...

OH!
LOOK OUT!!
KLAK
SHA
SORRY. I DIDN'T MEAN TO HIT YOU SO HARD!
Are you okay?
...
VEEN

YOU STAY OUTTA THIS!

IT'S NOT LIKE I REALLY SAVED YOU OR ANY-THING ...
BUT CONSIDER THIS PAYMENT FOR HELPING KOTOHA. WE'RE EVEN NOW.

HA! THIS HAS NOTHING TO DO WITH THAT! YOU CAN'T HAVE KOTOHA!!
YOU'RE LUCKY I'M A REASON-ABLE GUY!
Um ...
Don't I have any say in this?

THOOM
IF I WAS SERIOUS, MY HAYA—!
THOOM
THE HOUR OF RECKON-ING!
THOOM

THOOM
BA-BUMP BA-BUMP
BA-BUMP BA-BUMP
THOOM
ZSH ZSH ZSH
THE VIBRATIONS ARE GETTING CLOSER!
DON'T WORRY, GINCHI! YOU KNOW HOW IT GOES!
IT'LL BE OVER IN NO TIME.
AH...
THOOM

KANATE!!

KA...
KANATE !!
AAAAAH!!
NOOOOO!!

KANATE !!
THOOM
SHUDDER
...
HUH?
TREMBLE
TREMBLE
IT CAN'T BE...
THOOM
KLANG

KANATE !!
I'M COMING WITH YOU!!
GINCHI !!

CHAPTER 13
THE RECKONING
KANATE!!
GI...

GINCHI!!
GINCHI...
WHAT DO WE DO?!
THEY'LL DIE IF WE DON'T DO SOME-THING!
MASTER ARATA!!

MASTER ARATA?
I COULDN'T ...
HUH?
I COULDN'T MOVE!!

I'VE GOT...
...TO SAVE THEM!!

KOTOHA, ARE YOU ALL RIGHT?
THIS IS THE TUBE THAT SWALLOWED THEM. IF WE FOLLOW IT, IT SHOULD LEAD US TO TSU-TSUGA!
RIGHT!
IF WE'RE EVER GOING TO ESCAPE FROM GATOYA...
...I HAVE TO CONFRONT TSUTSUGA, WHETHER I LIKE IT OR NOT!
WHUP

KOTOHA! CAN YOU CLIMB DOWN?
HERE, GRAB MY...
AAH!
WHAM
SW
IP
AGH!
ZSH ZSH
ZSH ZSH

WOOSH
WAAAH!!
A water-slide?!
PLOP
SWUFF
WUMP
KOTOHA... I GAN'T BREATHE.
I'M SORRY! ARE YOU ALL RIGHT?!
BA-BUMP BA-BUMP
THAT FELT NICE ...

KRAK
AAH
Is Heaven punishing me?!
KWAK
KWAK
WAH!!
ARATA ?!
OH!

Hey...
OSOME!
AM I BACK IN THE MARKET-PLACE THEN?
WHAT IN THE WORLD ARE YOU DOING?!
ARE YOU ALL RIGHT, MASTER ARATA?
HUH?
OH, SO YOU FOUND THE GIRL YOU WERE LOOKING FOR, EH?
THAT'S GOOD. NOW COME ON DOWN.
NO THANKS! I HAVE TO HURRY AND FIND TSUTSUGA!
WHAT?!
ARE YOU OUT OF YOUR MIND?!
TWO BOYS GOT SWALLOWED UP IN THE LAST RECKONING, AND I NEED TO SAVE—
DON'T TALK CRAZY! FORGET THEM!!
YOU CAN'T DEFY A SHO AND HIS HAYAGAMI! IT'S SUICIDE!
SHE'S RIGHT! WE'RE JUST CRIMINAL SCUM TO HIM!
BUT...

IF I DON'T DO SOMETHING, WE'LL ALL CONTINUE TO LIVE IN FEAR OF TSUTSUGA'S JUDGMENT...
BUT AT LEAST WE'LL BE ALIVE!
UNDER THE RECKONING, ANY OF US CAN DIE AT ANY MOMENT!
BUT IT'S WRONG TO JUST THROW YOUR LIFE AWAY!
IT'S WRONG...
DO YOU WANT TO MAKE THAT GIRL NEXT TO YOU CRY?
THANKS FOR WORRYING ABOUT ME.
BUT... I HAVE TO GO! I CAN'T ABANDON THOSE TWO. AND I MADE A PROMISE TO THE PRINCESS.
OSOME...
WHAT?

DON'T WORRY! I'LL BE BACK FOR SURE!
BESIDES, I'M REALLY GOOD AT RUNNING AWAY!
ARATA...
DON'T WORRY! I'M GOING TOO!
...
GEEZ... DON'T SAY WE DIDN'T WARN YA.

BUT SHE WAS CONDEMNED TO THIS PLACE TOO.
MAYBE SHE WAS FRAMED LIKE I WAS...
I GUESS YOU REALLY SHOULDN'T JUDGE PEOPLE.

KANATE AND GINCHI ARE THIEVES...
...BUT ARE THEY REALLY EVIL?

AND THAT MAN...
"BUT I'M SURE YOU WILL SUCCEED."

WE'VE DESCENDED A LONG WAY. IT'S GETTING HOT...

HEY!

A LIGHT!

...!!

WHAT'S THAT SMELL?
POOR THINGS... THEY'RE SICK.
THEY MUST ISOLATE THEM HERE.
THAT MAN WAS RIGHT...
TO TSUTSUGA, PEOPLE HERE ARE JUST CRIMINAL SCUM.
...!
KOTOHA, HURRY!
SWUP

NGH ...
GINCHI ...
?!

GINCHI!! ARE YOU ALIVE?!
KANATE ...?
W-WHERE ARE WE?!
JUST WAIT, I'LL...
KREEK
ARE YOU CON-SCIOUS ...
...YOU FOOLISH CRIMINALS ?

WHO'S THERE?!
...WITH YOUR LIVES!
ZOH!
I AM TSUTSUGA, THE WARDEN OF GATOYA.
I... I CAN'T BREATHE...
W-WAIT! WE DIDN'T DO ANYTHING!
TSUTSUGA...
YOU DISGUSTING MISCREANTS WILL NOW PAY FOR YOUR CRIMES...
HMPH
THE WORM BEGS FOR ITS LIFE.
THROB
THROB

I SHALL GIVE YOU ONE CHANCE TO PROVE YOUR INNOCENCE.
DO SO, AND YOUR LIFE WILL BE SPARED.
YOU MUST FIGHT.
WAGER YOUR INNOCENCE ...
...AND FIGHT THE PERSON BEFORE YOUR EYES!

WHAT?
PROVE YOUR INNOCENCE BY WINNING, AND YOU'LL BE ALLOWED TO LEAVE GATOYA.
IF NOT, YOU'LL BE TORN APART!
KANATE ...
NOW FIGHT!!

KANATE, GINCHI, STAY ALIVE!
CHAPTER 14
TOTAL STRANGERS
FIGHT! WAGER YOUR LIVES TO PROVE YOUR INNOCENCE, BOTH OF YOU!
KANATE ...
OR DO YOU WANT TO DIE HERE?
...

HEH...
WHAT? YOU WANT US TO FIGHT TO THE DEATH?
Hmph
ME AND GINCHI?
NO WAY!!
HE'S LIKE A LITTLE BROTHER TO ME!!
KANATE ...
THEN YOU WILL BOTH PERISH.
KREEK
REFUSING TO PROVE YOUR INNOCENCE IS AN ADMISSION OF GUILT!
KREEK
UNH...
KREEK
ST...

STOP!!!
SHUP
SHUDD
NOW TAKE UP YOUR WEAPONS!
NO...
FIGHT!

WHAP
STAND UP, GINCHI! WE HAVE NO CHOICE!
THERE'S NO SENSE IN BOTH OF US DYING HERE!
FWIP
FWIP
AT LEAST THE ONE WHO LIVES GETS TO LEAVE THE ISLAND!
KANATE!!
NO, I CAN'T FIGHT YOU!!
HERE I COME, GINCHI!!

TMP
YES, EXCELLENT ...
?!
KANATE?! GINCHI?!
IF YOU WANT TO PROVE YOUR INNO-CENCE ...
...AND LEAVE GATOYA, THEN FIGHT!
IF YOU WANT TO LIVE, KILL YOUR OPPONENT !!
!!

THAT'S TOO CRUEL!!
I HAVE TO STOP THEM! STAY HERE, KOTOHA!
MASTER ARATA!
TMP
WHAP
WHO ARE YOU?!
TSUTSUGA, MAKE THEM STOP!! THEY'RE FRIENDS!!
SHWOFF
IF YOU INTERFERE WITH MY JUDGMENT, YOU WILL BE EXECUTED IMMEDIATE-LY.
TSUTSUGA? IS HE INSIDE THAT MASS OF TUBES?!
HUMANS ARE ALL ALIKE.

THEY ONLY LOVE THEM-SELVES! THEY ONLY WANT TO SAVE THEM-SELVES!
GASP
THOSE TWO ARE THE SAME ...
"I DON'T WANT TO BE ASSOCIATED WITH A GUY LIKE THAT."
"THAT'S COLD. I THOUGHT YOU TWO WERE FRIENDS."
I NEVER REALLY LIKED THAT GUY.
KLANK
YOU GUYS TOO?
WHAT ARE YOU DOING?

IF YOU WANT TO BE SPARED, THEN SETTLE THIS QUICKLY!
DON'T HOLD BACK, YOU SCUM!!
"MOMMY..."
"DADDY..."
"THAT'S THE BRAT WE KIDNAPPED YESTERDAY."
"KANATE, YOU'RE IN CHARGE OF HIM. TEACH HIM HOW TO STEAL LIKE WE DO."
Heh.
YEAH, WE'RE TOTAL STRANGERS.
HURRY UP AND KILL HIM!!

WHUP
SORRY, GINCHI!
THIS ONE'S GONNA FINISH YOU!!
!!

"SO YOUR NAME'S GINCHI, HUH? WHATCHA GOT THERE?"

"MY MOM'S RING..."

"WELL, TAKE GOOD CARE OF IT. SOMEDAY I'LL TAKE YOU BACK TO YOUR MOM..."

"...CAN GO FREE."
KANATE!!
"YOU ...
THE DUEL IS OVER. THIS BOY IS THE CRIMINAL, AND...
Ah ...

THWAP
...YOU!
WHAT?
!!
I PASS JUDGMENT ON CRIMES! AND YOU JUST COMMITTED THE CRIME ...
...OF MURDER !!
RGH...

DAMN IT! WHAT IS THIS?!

GINCHI !!
WHAT?! YOU DARE TO INTERFERE ?!
I CAN'T BELIEVE THIS... IS THIS WHAT THE RECKONING IS?!
YOU PIT TWO PRISONERS AGAINST EACH OTHER, AND THEN YOU EXECUTE THE SURVIVOR ANYWAY ?!

IS THAT HOW YOU TEST THE HUMAN HEART?!
PEOPLE AREN'T YOUR PLAY-THINGS!!
ENOUGH OF YOUR PRATTLE, SCUM!!
SHOOM
WHAM

COME OUT HERE, TSU-TSUGA!! YOU COWARD!!
DO YOU REALLY PRESUME TO THWART ME?!
THEN ...
WHUD
WHUP

HE'S NOT HERE?!
MASTER ARATA!!

CHAPTER 15
KAMUI
MASTER ARATA!!
NGH ...

ZANG
AGH...
SWIP
YOU SQUIRMING LITTLE ...
TSUTSUGA, WHERE ARE YOU ...?
SWIP
AGH!

YOU WORM! I'LL TEAR YOU TO PIECES!!
MAS-TER ARATA!!
UNGH...
AH!
KANATE?!
HANG IN THERE!!
UNH...
AAAAAH!!
RRMMMMMM
HUH?! THE GROUND IS TREM-BLING!

KROOOOM
AAAGH!
BOOM
AGH!
KRASH
THE RECKON-ING AGAIN?!
OW!
NGH!

SHEEN
GRAAAH!!
SOME-BODY'S RUNNING UP THERE?!
Wow...
HEY, ISN'T THAT THE NEW KID?!

DN
GATOYA ...
A DREARY ISLAND, AS USUAL.
And so humid...
LORD KANNAGI! YOU HAVE BUSINESS WITH THE BOY WHO KILLED THE PRINCESS?
WHAT INTER-ESTS ME IS HIS HAYA-GAMI.
TSUTSUGA IS A REBELLIOUS SHO WHO DOESN'T BELONG WITH THE TWELVE SHINSHO ...

IF HE'S ALREADY PASSED JUDGMENT ON ARATA AND MANAGED TO KILL HIM...
...THEN THAT'S IT FOR THAT HAYA-GAMI.
KRROOOM
NA
M
?!
OSOME! IT'S TERRIBLE!
THAT BOY IS FIGHTING WARDEN TSUTSUGA!
ARATA ?!
IT'S NO USE!
AT THIS RATE, I'LL BE KILLED !!
IF ONLY I COULD FIND TSUTSUGA AND STOP HIS HAYAGAMI ...

RRMMM
HUFF HUFF
STOP HIS HAYA-GAMI?
I CAN'T EVEN USE MY OWN HAYAGAMI!
WHAT'S THE MATTER, BRAT?
AREN'T YOU GOING TO USE THAT RUSTY OLD SWORD?
SHK
!!

WHAM
ARATA !!

IT HURTS... I CAN'T BREATHE...
IT'S NO USE.
THIS IS IMPOSSIBLE...
MASTER ...
!!
NGH...
IT WILL ALL BE OVER SOON.
YOU WILL DIE WITH THE OTHERS!!
MASTER ARATA!!

MASTER ARATA!!

KO... TO... HA...

I'M SORRY. I CAN'T ...

"I'M SURE YOU WILL SUCCEED."

IT'S... IMPOSSIBLE...

"WHY ...

"...DID YOU MAKE SUCH A BIG PROMISE?"

I...
GRP
H-HE'S STANDING!
GROOOOO
HAYA-GAMI!!
I'M BEGGING YOU!!

I...
APPEAR!!

I'M NOT GOING TO LET THEM DOWN!!

AH!
THAT'S ...

KAMUI ?!
THEN THAT IS A HAYA-GAMI... YOU-!
YOU ARE A SHO ?!

CHAPTER 16
AWAKENING
HE'S A SHO?!
...
SHUU
TO THINK THAT THAT BOY ...
THERE'S NO DOUBT ABOUT IT! THAT LIGHT IS KAMUI !!
INCRED-IBLE! HE'S FLOAT-ING!
MASTER ARATA!

HE'S A SHO!
KANATE! IT'S AMAZING! HE'S A SHO!! HE'S BLASTING TSUTSUGA'S TUBES WITH HIS HAYAGAMI!
SHO...
KOTOHA! KANATE, GINCHI, ARE YOU ALL RIGHT?

KRAK
KRAK
!!
AH
RUN FOR IT, YOU GUYS!!
OVER THERE!
TSUTSUGA ...!

HUH?!
AH...

DOOM
THAT'S... WARDEN TSU-TSUGA ?!
H-HE'S AN OLD GEEZER!!
TMP
I NEVER EXPECTED SOMEONE LIKE YOU TO BE A SHO...
YOU'RE TSU-TSUGA ?!
WHY DOES HE LOOK LIKE THAT?
UNH ...
UNGH ...
WM
A HAYAGAMI ?!

IT CAN'T BE...
NO, IT'S TRUE!! BUT HOW?
UNH...
TAP
ARE YOU IN PAIN?
WHAP
ZANG
!!
HUH?!

TSU-TSUGA?!

"REPENT AND RE-HABILITATE ON THIS ISLAND.

"ACCEPT THE LIGHT OF SANIWA, MY HAYAGAMI. WHEN YOUR HEART HAS CHANGED, YOU MAY LEAVE THE ISLAND OF YOUR OWN ACCORD."

"YOU ERRED AND KILLED A MAN.

"YOU'RE AN OLD FRIEND, BUT A CRIME IS A CRIME."

"NO ONE IS BORN A CRIMI-NAL."

"WHAT DID YOU WANT TO SEE ME ABOUT?"

"PLEASE, TSUTSUGA! LET ME LEAVE THIS PLACE!"

"IT'S BEEN TEN YEARS ... WE'RE OLD FRIENDS!"

"NOT THIS AGAIN... IT'S HARD FOR ME TOO, BUT YOUR HEART MUST CHANGE ..."

"DIE!!
"YOU THINK THAT BEING A SHO GIVES YOU THE RIGHT TO PASS JUDGMENT ON OTHERS!
"YOU CAN TAKE YOUR HAYA-GAMI ...
"...AND DIE RIGHT HERE!!"
"WHY, YOU ...!"

"I BELIEVED IN YOU...
"...AND YOU BETRAYED ME!!"
"PEOPLE NEVER CHANGE."
"VERY WELL. THEN INSTEAD OF A GOD, THIS HAYAGAMI WILL BE A DEMON."

AND I WILL USE ITS DEMONIC POWERS TO IMPRISON CRIMINALS HERE FOREVER!!
TSU-TSUGA...
YOU SHOULDN'T READ A PERSON'S MIND WITHOUT PERMIS-SION.
BUT I DOUBT THAT YOU CAN UNDERSTAND MY FEELINGS ANYWAY.
HURRY IT UP AND FINISH ME OFF!
Y-YEAH!!
KILL HIM!!
WE MAY BE CRIMINALS, BUT WE DIDN'T DESERVE WHAT THAT FIEND PUT US THROUGH!!
AAAAAH
DO IT!
DO IT!

SWUP

SUBSIDE.

ZANG

?!

!!
WHAT ...?

WHAT ARE YOU DOING?!
YOU'LL BE KILLED!!
WELL, I CAN'T...
...LEAVE HIM LIKE THIS...
(SHHK)
H-HEY... HE'S...
IS HE TRYING TO SAVE TSUTSUGA?!
DON'T BE A FOOL! YOU CAN'T WIN OVER A HAYAGAMI THAT HAS TURNED INTO A DEMON.
SHHK SHHK
SHHK SHHK
?!

HATE ...
AGH !
RESENT-MENT ...
THAT VOICE... IS IT TSUTSUGA'S?! HIS HAYAGAMI'S ?!
THWAK
YOU LIKE PAIN, HUH, HINO-HARA!
K-KADO-WAKI?!
HATE HIM. HE IS YOUR ENEMY.
BUT YOUR WORST ENEMY IS...
AH!
YOU KIND OF OVERDID IT WITH THE GLUE.
THAT'S COLD. I THOUGHT YOU TWO WERE FRIENDS.
UNGH ...
MY... HEART ...
...FEELS LIKE IT'S GOING TO BURST!

ARE YOU KIDDING?
I NEVER REALLY LIKED THAT GUY.
SUGURU...!!
WHY?!
"I NEVER REALLY LIKED THAT GUY."
PUNISH ALL TRAITORS!!
YOU ARE JUST LIKE ME...
...DESTINED TO BECOME A DEMON.
...
NO.

DESPITE THAT ...
...I CONSIDERED HIM MY FRIEND!!

I'M SURE OF THAT...
...EVEN NOW...
I DON'T UNDER-STAND IT!!
I DON'T UNDER-STAND PEOPLE AT ALL!!
BUT YOU CAN'T STAY HERE ALL ALONE IN A PLACE LIKE THIS!!
WHAT GOOD IS HATING PEOPLE AND SUFFERING?!
HOLD ON!! I'M GOING TO HELP YOU... RIGHT NOW!
SWF
UNH!

HE PULLED IT OUT!!

HUFF
IT'S OUT!
HUFF
TSUTSUGA ...
HUFF
HUFF
CHAPTER 17
THE GREAT SHINSHO
DOES THAT FEEL BETTER?

WHY?
HUH?
WHY WOULD YOU GO TO SUCH LENGTHS TO HELP ME?
HOW DID YOU WIN OVER THE DEMON POWER OF A HAYA-GAMI?
I DON'T KNOW WHY...
...BUT EARLIER WHEN I LOOKED INTO YOUR PAST, I FELT A PAIN IN MY HEART.
I WAS JUST LIKE YOU. SOMEONE I TRUSTED BETRAYED ME, AND I WAS REALLY ANGRY.
BUT I WANT TO HAVE FAITH IN HIM...
WHEN YOU KEEP TESTING PEOPLE, YOU'LL ALWAYS BE DISAPPOINTED IN THEM.
I GUESS I MIGHT'VE BEEN LIKE THAT TOO.

WE WANT TO FORGIVE THEM, DON'T WE?
BUT I'M STARTING TO REALIZE PEOPLE DON'T ALWAYS LET YOU DOWN...
JUST NOW, I WANTED YOU TO REALIZE THAT TOO.
YOU CAN'T STAY HERE ALL ALONE IN A PLACE LIKE THIS!!
WHAT GOOD IS HATING PEOPLE AND SUFFER-ING?!

Arata
THE LEGEND

IT MUST'VE BEEN ...
...SO HARD FOR YOU.
AH ...
SWUP
THIS IS SO EMBARRASSING!

SHEEN
THE HAYAGAMI, IT...!
THAT IS THE TRUE FORM OF THE HAYAGAMI SANIWA.
YOU SAY YOUR NAME IS ARATA...
I WISH I HAD MET YOU LONG AGO ...
EH?
I AM A SHO WHO BECAME A DEMON, A CRIMINAL WHO LOST HIS HEART.
I DON'T DESERVE TO WIELD THAT HAYAGAMI ANY LONGER.
SHH
BUT I KNOW THAT YOU WILL WIELD SANIWA WITH JUSTICE.
?!
FWASH

?!
ZHEEEN
HAYAGAMI SANIWA ...

SUBMIT TO THIS GREAT SHO.
MY SOUL WILL BE ONE WITH THE GREAT HAYAGAMI.
VWMSH
?!

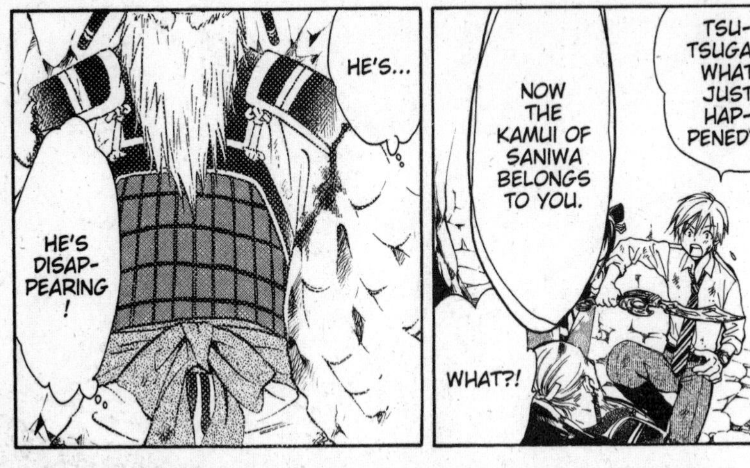
TSU-TSUGA!! WHAT JUST HAPPENED?!
NOW THE KAMUI OF SANIWA BELONGS TO YOU.
WHAT?!
HE'S...
HE'S DISAPPEARING!

TSUTSUGA?!
MY HAYAGAMI AND I HAVE GONE INTO YOU. MY PURPOSE HERE IS DONE.
FROM NOW ON, I WILL LIVE ON INSIDE YOUR HAYAGAMI.

LET ME BEAR WITNESS, SHO...
AS THE NEW WARDEN, RESTORE THE PEACE AND ORDER THAT ONCE PREVAILED IN GATOYA.
APPEAR!
FWASH

SANIWA!!

LORD KAN-NAGI!
UNTIL WE'VE IDENTIFIED WHO ATTACKED US WITH THAT BEAM OF LIGHT, IT'S TOO DANGEROUS TO LAND!
I ALREADY KNOW WHO'S BEHIND IT!
ARATA!
HOW DARE HE ATTACK MY SHIP?!
SHK
SHK

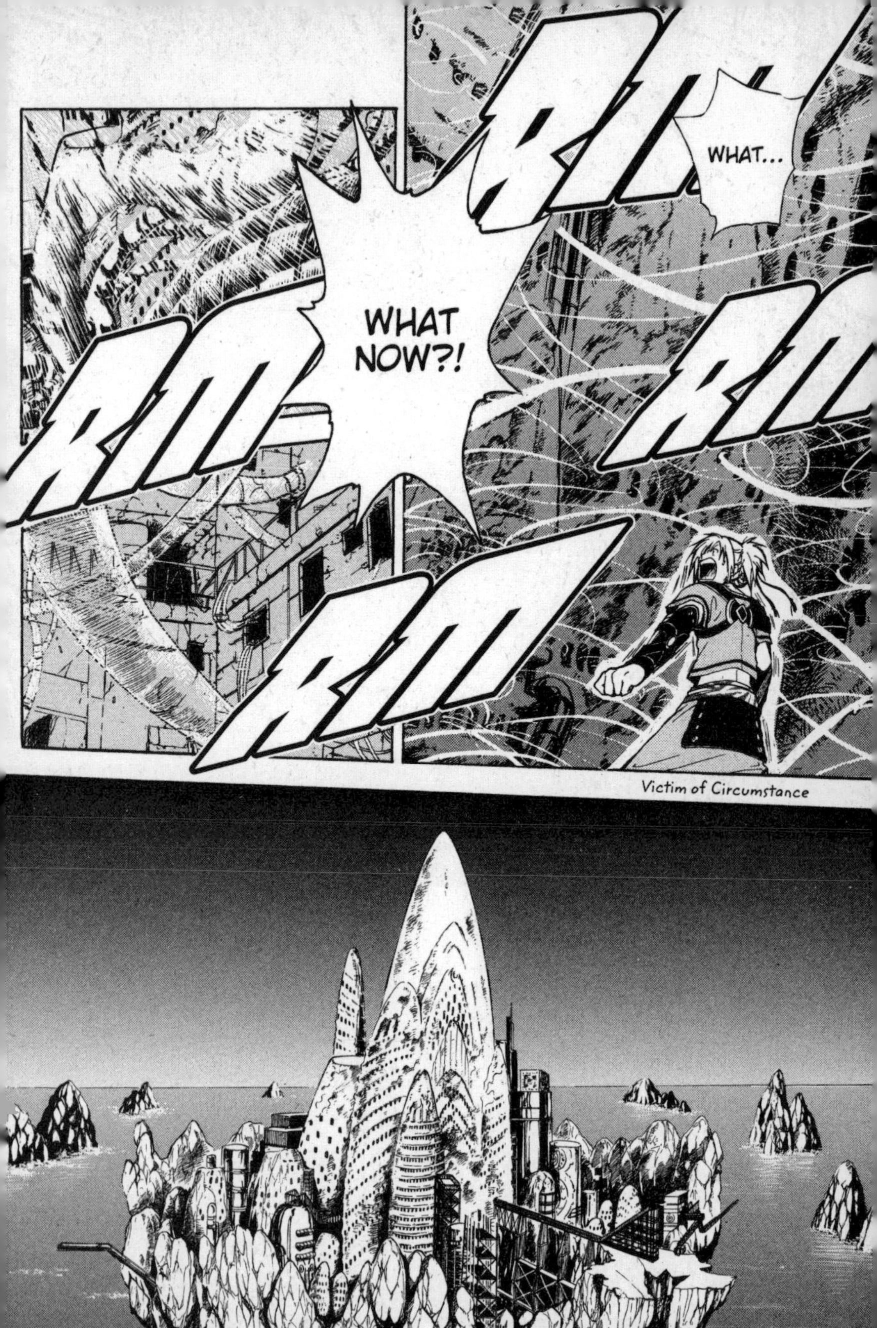
WHAT...
WHAT NOW?!
Victim of Circumstance

LOOK! THE CLIFFS ARE... SINKING?!
SWUP
SUBSIDE!
OH!

IT'S BACK...
...TO HOW IT WAS BEFORE!
WHAT'S THIS?
HEY, LOOK DOWN THERE!
IT'S THE MEN WHO WERE TAKEN DURING THE HOUR OF RECKONING!
THEY'RE ALL ALIVE !!
Unh ...
AH!
MASAHI !!

O...
OSOME ...?
MASAHI!! YOU'RE ALIVE! I'M COMING FOR YOU!!
YOU'RE WONDERFUL, ARATA!!
SWUFF
O-OSOME ?!
HE'S ALIVE!!
WE...
WE WERE SENT HERE FOR ATTEMPTING TO END OUR LIVES TOGETHER ...
THANK YOU, ARATA!! THANK GOODNESS WE'RE ALL ALIVE!
...
HEY...
LOOKS LIKE ANOTHER SHO HAS ARRIVED!
BZZ

IT'S ONE OF THE TWELVE SHINSHO!
TOMP
ARATA!!
WHERE ARE YOU?!
KAN-NAGI?!
WHAT'S HE DOING HERE?!
DID I DO SOME-THING?!
EITHER WAY WE HAVE TO FLEE, MASTER ARATA!
THIS WAY.
AAAAAGH!!
COME TO OUR HIDEOUT.
KANATE?!
IT'S TEN LEVELS UP. YOU ALREADY KNOW THE WAY.

HURRY AND GO, ARATA.
TSU-TSUGA...
IF YOU'RE LOOKING FOR THE SHO, HE'S IN THE COURTYARD AT THE VERY BOTTOM.
WARDEN TSUTSUGA WAS DEFEATED, AND...
WHAT?!
MAKE WAY FOR THEM!!
KANATE! WHY ARE WE GOING BACK?!
IF THE WARPED AREA CHANGED TO HOW IT WAS BEFORE...
...THEN OUR PLACE IS PROBABLY...
TMP
OH!!

THAT ROOM WAS INSIDE A SHIP?!
THEN WE CAN USE IT TO GET OFF THE ISLAND!!
THANKS TO ARATA, MAYBE WE CAN ALL LEAVE GATOYA!
TSU-TSUGA!!

WHERE'S ARATA?!
I'LL KILL HIM!!
ARATA'S GONE!
SO IT'S KAN-NAGI OF THE TWELVE SHIN-SHO.
WHAT DO YOU WANT WITH THAT INNOCENT BOY?
YOU ...!
TSU-TSUGA ?!
WHUP
YOUR APPEAR-ANCE... DON'T TELL ME YOU SUBMITTED TO HIM!
WHY ...?
HEH HEH...

SOMEDAY YOU'LL UNDERSTAND. THAT BOY IS STRONG.
AND THAT'S THE HAYAGAMI THAT WILL RULE OVER THIS WORLD.
TSU-TSUGA, YOU DIDN'T EXECUTE THE PRISONERS AFTER ALL.
I WONDER IF OSOME AND THE REST WILL BE ABLE TO GET OFF THE ISLAND
I WONDER IF HE WAS WATCHING...
"I'M SURE YOU WILL SUCCEED."
YES! I CAN DO IT! MAYBE HERE I CAN CHANGE!!

WE'RE OUT!!
MASTER ARATA, PLEASE DON'T FALL OVER-BOARD.
BY THE WAY, GINCHI, WHERE IS THIS SHIP HEADED?
Uh...
DON'T WORRY. I KNOW WHERE WE'RE GOING!
KLINK
TO THE CAPITAL, WHERE THE PRINCESS IS!!
KRK

ARATA: THE LEGEND 2 (THE END)

TALKING ABOUT ARATA: THE LEGEND

アラタカンガタル。

PANIC IN THE HINOHARA HOUSEHOLD!

Afterwards, a huge marital spat ensued.

ARATA PANICS TOO!!

↑Improvised drawing

TO BE CONTINUED...

CONCEPT SKETCHES MADE PUBLIC
①
ARATA HINOHARA (HERO)
BEIGE
(15 YEARS OLD, FIRST-YEAR IN HIGH SCHOOL)
ABOUT 170 CM!
SKIN
RAY
LET'S START WITH THE HEROES FIRST. MANY WERE STARTLED WHEN I SHOWED THEM ARATA AS THE MAIN CHARACTER IN THE FIRST CHAPTER... THIS IS PART OF THE CONCEPT I SHOWED THE EDITOR.
ARATA OF THE HIME CLAN
BACK

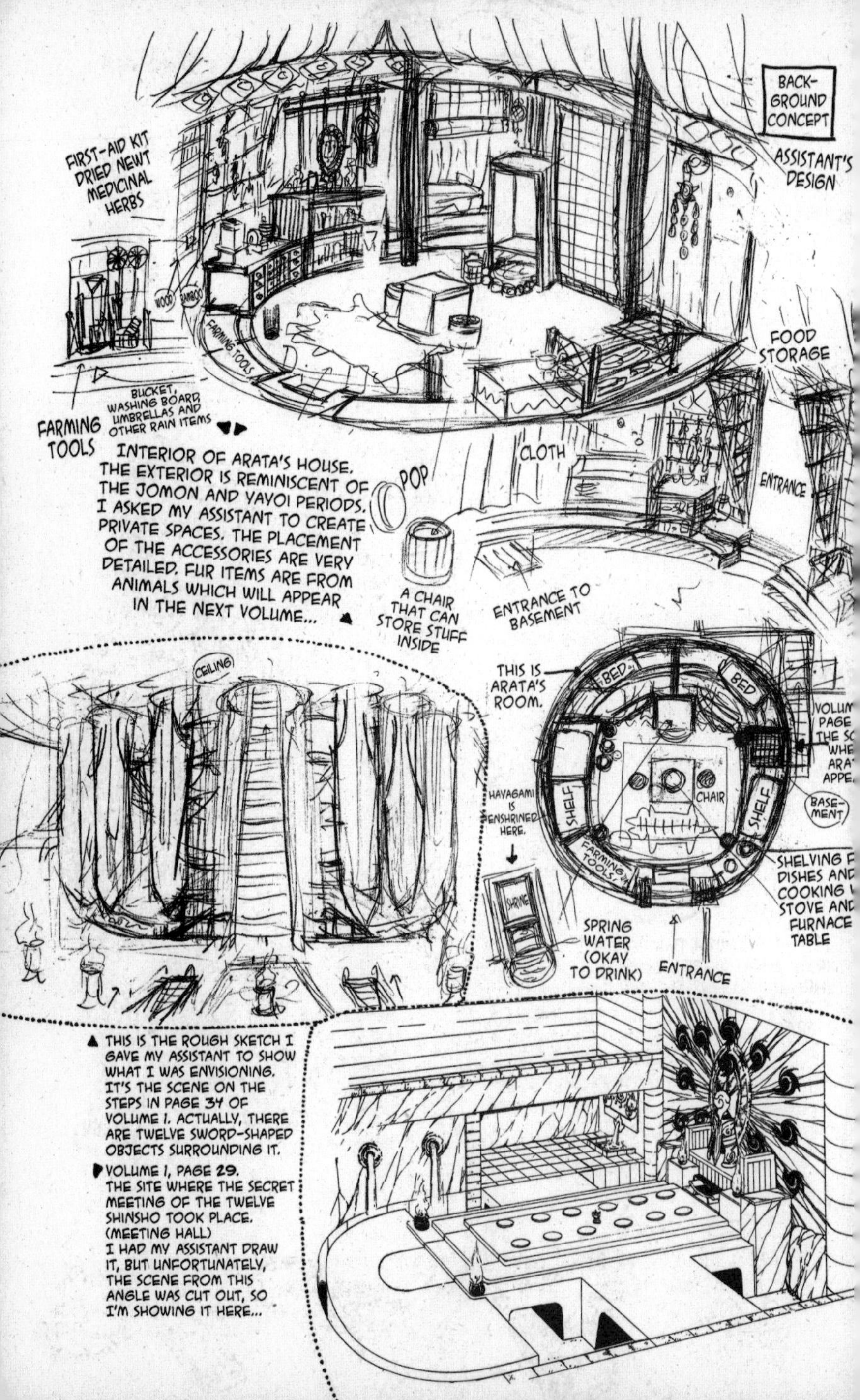
BACK-GROUND CONCEPT
ASSISTANT'S DESIGN
FIRST-AID KIT
DRIED NEWT
MEDICINAL HERBS
WOOD
BAMBOO
FARMING TOOLS
BUCKET, WASHING BOARD, UMBRELLAS AND OTHER RAIN ITEMS
FARMING TOOLS
FOOD STORAGE
INTERIOR OF ARATA'S HOUSE. THE EXTERIOR IS REMINISCENT OF THE JOMON AND YAYOI PERIODS. I ASKED MY ASSISTANT TO CREATE PRIVATE SPACES. THE PLACEMENT OF THE ACCESSORIES ARE VERY DETAILED. FUR ITEMS ARE FROM ANIMALS WHICH WILL APPEAR IN THE NEXT VOLUME...
POP
CLOTH
ENTRANCE
A CHAIR THAT CAN STORE STUFF INSIDE
ENTRANCE TO BASEMENT
CEILING
THIS IS ARATA'S ROOM.
BED
BED
SHELF
CHAIR
SHELF
BASE-MENT
HAYAGAMI IS ENSHRINED HERE.
SHRINE
FARMING TOOLS
SHELVING F
DISHES AND
COOKING
STOVE AND
FURNACE
TABLE
SPRING WATER (OKAY TO DRINK)
ENTRANCE
THIS IS THE ROUGH SKETCH I GAVE MY ASSISTANT TO SHOW WHAT I WAS ENVISIONING. IT'S THE SCENE ON THE STEPS IN PAGE 34 OF VOLUME 1. ACTUALLY, THERE ARE TWELVE SWORD-SHAPED OBJECTS SURROUNDING IT.
VOLUME 1, PAGE 29. THE SITE WHERE THE SECRET MEETING OF THE TWELVE SHINSHO TOOK PLACE. (MEETING HALL) I HAD MY ASSISTANT DRAW IT, BUT UNFORTUNATELY, THE SCENE FROM THIS ANGLE WAS CUT OUT, SO I'M SHOWING IT HERE...

ROUGH SKETCH OF KANATE AND GINCHI'S ROOM (INSIDE THE SHIP)
ENTRANCE AND EXIT
WINDOW
IT'S A ROUGH SKETCH, SO MAYBE A LITTLE HARD TO FIGURE OUT, BUT THE OUTSIDE DOOR...
I HADN'T TOLD MY ASSISTANT KANATE AND GINCHI'S NAMES AT THIS POINT. (HEH.)
YOUR ROOM
MY ROOM
PIPE
THE SETTING FOR THE BATTLE SCENE BETWEEN TSUTSUGA AND ARATA. (ROUGH) BECAUSE GATOYA IS SUPPOSED TO BE A PLACE WHERE THE SPACE IS WARPED, EVERYTHING IS TOPSY-TURVY. (I WAS IMAGINING SOMETHING LIKE BLOOD VESSELS OR THE INSIDE OF A BODY HERE.) IT'S TSUTSUGA'S INTERNAL SELF (WITHIN HIS HEART).
ARATA JUMPED OVER THIS... I WOULD FALL!!
1.5 METERS
PIPE
THIS IS LINKED TO THE SCENE WHERE KANATE AND GINCHI HAD TO FIGHT.

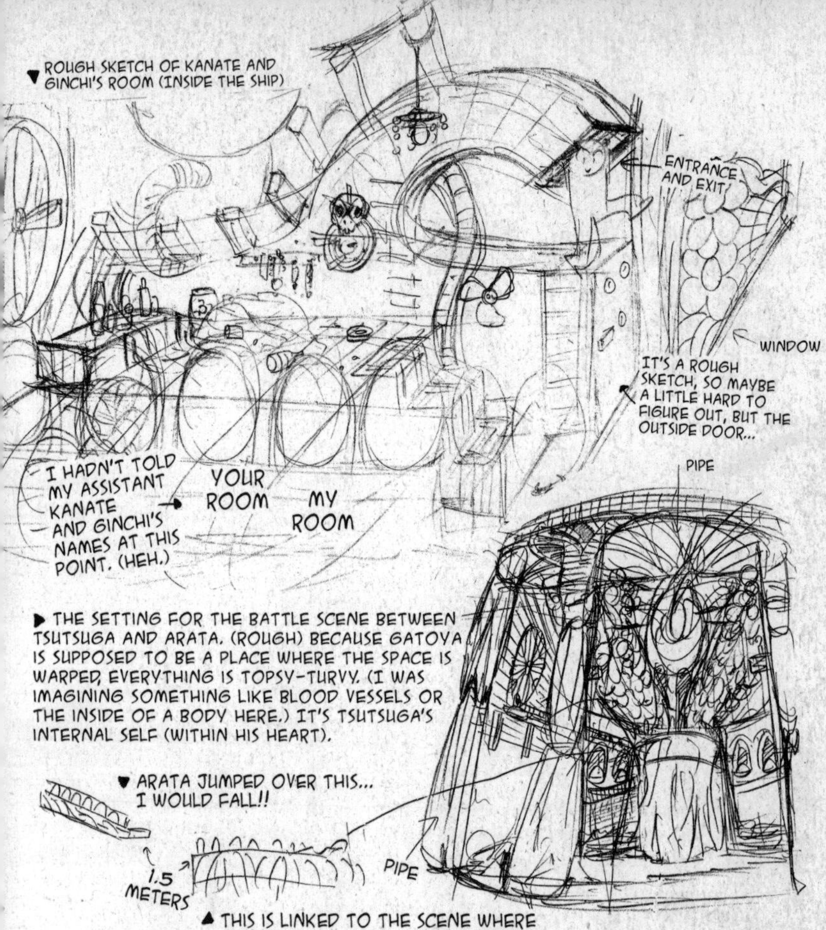

OH WELL, SPACE IS RUNNING OUT, SO IT'S ON TO VOLUME 3.
I HAVE LOTS OF CONCEPT SKETCHES, SO I'LL BE INCLUDING THEM AT THE END OF THE VOLUMES. NATURALLY, I CAN'T INCLUDE ALL OF THEM... MORE IMPORTANTLY, PLEASE LOOK FORWARD TO THE CONTINUING STORY. I MADE TSUTSUGA, WHO APPEARS IN THIS VOLUME, AN OLDER MAN IN ORDER TO JUXTAPOSE HIM WITH THE YOUNG ARATA... LIKE HE'S SOMEONE ARATA MIGHT HAVE BECOME IN THE FUTURE. I WANTED TO CREATE A SCENE WHERE TSUTSUGA COULD ENTRUST THE FUTURE TO SOMEONE WHO HAS A FUTURE AHEAD OF HIM. (BY THE WAY, BOTH "GATOYA" AND "TSUTSUGA" MEAN "JAIL.")
I'VE BEEN WORKING ON TWO OTHER SERIES (IN DIFFERENT GENRES) AND AFTER MUCH DISCUSSION, IT'S BEEN DECIDED THAT ONE OF THEM, *FUSHIGI YÛGI: GENBU KAIDEN*, WILL RESUME SERIALIZATION IN A YEAR IN **2010**...
TO THOSE WHO WERE LOOKING FORWARD TO THAT, MY APOLOGIES!!!
BUT I REALLY WANT TO RESUME IT UNDER THE BEST CONDITIONS, SO PLEASE BE PATIENT...
BUT THERE WILL BE LOTS OF *ARATA: THE LEGEND* COMICS! I WILL CONTINUE TO DO MY BEST!!

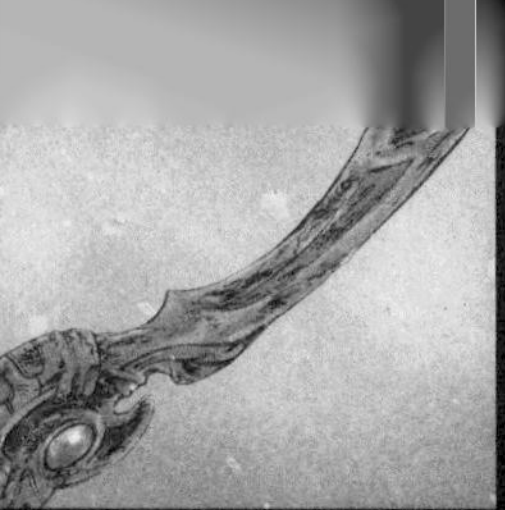

The setting for this work is based on ancient Japan (sort of), but I've randomly mixed different eras. It's very difficult to create a fantasy that isn't based on a specific time and place. It's not like creating a video game where you have lots and lots of people working on it. When I have ideas, I only have a few assistants to help me develop them. So like Arata, we're often left wondering what comes next! Whenever I can, I'll try to keep using settings like oceans, skies and plains. That may not always be possible, but I'll do my best.

–Yuu Watase

AUTHOR BIO

Born March 5 in Osaka, Yuu Watase debuted in the *Shôjo Comic* manga anthology in 1989. She won the 43rd Shogakukan Manga Award with *Ceres: Celestial Legend*. One of her most famous works is *Fushigi Yûgi*, a series that has inspired the prequel *Fushigi Yûgi: Genbu Kaiden*. In 2008, *Arata: The Legend* started serialization in *Shonen Sunday*.

ARATA: THE LEGEND
Volume 2
Shonen Sunday Edition

Story and Art by Yuu WATASE

© 2009 Yuu WATASE/Shogakukan
All rights reserved.
Original Japanese edition "ARATAKANGATARI"
published by SHOGAKUKAN Inc.

English Adaptation: Lance Caselman
Translation: JN Productions
Touch-up Art & Lettering: Rina Mapa
Design: Frances O. Liddell
Editor: Amy Yu

VP, Production: Alvin Lu
VP, Sales & Product Marketing: Gonzalo Ferreyra
VP, Creative: Linda Espinosa
Publisher: Hyoe Narita

The stories, characters and incidents mentioned in this publication are entirely fictional.

No portion of this book may be reproduced or transmitted in any form or by any means without written permission from the copyright holders.

Printed in the U.S.A.

Published by VIZ Media, LLC
P.O. Box 77010
San Francisco, CA 94107

10 9 8 7 6 5 4 3 2 1
First printing, June 2010

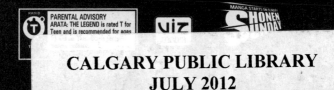

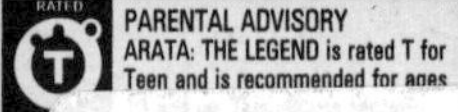
RATED
T
PARENTAL ADVISORY
ARATA: THE LEGEND is rated T for
Teen and is recommended for ages

viz

MANGA STARTS ON SUNDAY
SHONEN SUNDAY

CALGARY PUBLIC LIBRARY
JULY 2012